A Collection of Whimsical Tales

Adventures with Ragweed

By Linda Lou Crosby

Illustrated by Andy Atkins

Neon Lines
Montana
Printed in USA

This is a work of fiction. Names, characters, places, and incidents are the product of the author's imagination. Names of actual persons, places, and characters are incidental to the plot, and are not intended to change the entirely fictional character of the work.

Copyright © 2013 by Linda Lou Crosby

All rights reserved. Published and Printed in the United States.

http://neonlines.com/

Neon Lines, Montana

Book Design by Laura Dobbins
Illustrated by Andy Atkins
Cover Design by Laura Dobbins
Cover Illustration by Andy Atkins

Cataloging-in-Publication Data is on file with the Library of Congress.

ISBN:

978-0615895383

MANUFACTURED IN THE UNITED STATES OF AMERICA

First Edition

This book is dedicated to ...

When I thought of why I was writing Ragweed, I knew it was partly because my husband told me I needed to do it. Probably because he was hoping that if I wrote these stories down, I would quit coming up with half-witted ideas that get him involved in escapades that have strange outcomes.

But I assure you that is NOT the case.

I write and am dedicating Ragweed to my children, grandchildren and great grandchildren. They are the true joys of our universe, as they still see life as a kaleidoscope of possibilities. With the stories of Ragweed I wish to add a bit of the whimsical to their lives…..forever.

TABLE of Contents

Introduction... 7

Ragweed grows a Garden 9

Ragweed fries Eggs... 15

Ragweed helps with Chores 21

Ragweed goes to Mexico.. 29

Ragweed makes Compost... 41

Ragweed mows the Lawn 47

Ragweed builds a Float... 53

Ragweed and her Racket 59

Ragweed wears a Uniform 71

Ragweed rides a Horse 79

Linda Lou Crosby

Introduction

Ragweed grew out of my experiences; the little girl part of me that peered out and saw a world of entertaining adventures before her. I don't think my folks always saw things the way I did…the lawn became an opportunity for crop rotation, or a sidewalk on a hot day showed potential for cooking breakfast…things like that. And I am quite sure that the results of some of my experiments were at times life altering for my parents.

I do think it did us all good (although my parents might not be in total agreement) to attempt the impossible, to take a chance at the improbable, and to look at life through a different view.

Ragweed is not me. She is a part of me though. As I began to write Ragweed's stories, her life took on a life of its own, with a wealthy Moms and Pops, who are busy doing their thing, which gives Ragweed time to do hers. They live at a grandiose estate, because I thought that would be fun.

Ragweed has a best friend Marney, a summary of all the very best friends I have had and do have, and who patiently endure some of my quirkier ideas and live to tell about it. And then there are the neighbors; a compilation of fun and fascinating neighbors I had as a child that popped up, as the character of Ragweed began to go on her own merry way.

I would say that Ragweed is a tribute to the whimsical part of each of us. She is committed to adventure without necessarily allowing for consequences. She loves life and is dedicated to the proposition that all adventures are created equal, even if they don't turn out that way. And she has a unique view of the world, which allows for unlimited possibilities.

I invite Ragweed's readers to venture along with her, and enjoy her escapades for what they are. My husband has referred to me as a "loveable pain in the neck". May Ragweed bring that fun into your lives as well.

Ragweed grows a Garden

It was a lovely spring day. Clouds circled slowly over the Santa Inez mountains. The blue sky was really blue. And although Ragweed was a mere five years old, she was old enough to recognize that her parents' perfectly manicured lawn and garden was boring. It lacked luster. It lacked…well, plants.

Ragweed loved Lupines. They popped up unannounced in the spring, all purple and fun. You never knew where they might be, but you knew they were coming any day. Why people mowed down perfectly good flowers, that smelled delicious, and put in camellia bushes, that were dull and didn't smell at all, and a lawn, was an astonishing thing to Ragweed. And the gardener that came weekly to mow grass, pull weeds, and generally flatten the landscape was completely convinced that anything uninvited was "outta there."

The gardener, Carl, was a nice enough guy, but he lacked vision. He apparently thought that life consisted of mowing anything uninvited down. In his serious minded fashion, his job was to mow things. Once Ragweed had "dropped" a stuffed bear underneath the kitchen window, just to see what would happen. Sure enough, it got mowed. Unfortunately for Carl, it was a windy day, and the stuffing flew everywhere. Although that was fairly satisfying to Ragweed, something else needed to be done. Ragweed's manicured parents would never understand. They thought lawns were great. They never walked on them, or had picnics on them, or even noticed them really…unless there was an issue of some sort, like a brown spot, which Carl would never allow.

Ragweed hated lawns. They were ridiculous in her eyes. Once they were grown, and mowed, then you weren't allowed to run and play on them anymore. So what was the point? Of course, back East you have to mow the grass, otherwise you wouldn't be able to find your home in about a month. But that was different. That was about survival. This was Southern California. Grass just wasn't a normal thing. Yet people thought nothing about how much watering it took to keep the grass green and growing, only to turn around and mow it down.

One day, for no apparent reason that Ragweed could fathom, Moms and Pops told Ragweed she could have a little part of the yard for her very own first ever garden.

"I would like to plant a garden," Ragweed told her parents, who lent their support to the idea even providing seeds and tools. Ragweed planted a few things, and ran out everyday to see how the seeds were doing.

Relatives and friends of the family were surprised with Ragweed's interest in the garden, as many believed her to be allergic to plants and flowers. After all, Ragweed got her nickname because she sneezed so often. Her parents thought it was allergies. Little did anyone know it was foolishness that spurred the symptoms – for instance when asked to wash dishes, Ragweed had a sneezing fit. And after Ragweed had sneezed all over the dishes, no one wanted her help anyhow. Being given orders of any kind also seemed to bring about a sneezing attack, like "It's bedtime." Ragweed's sneezing would clear out the den, then she had the TV to herself for the night.

Truth be told, Ragweed loved the outdoors, the smell of the earth, the way each wildflower perfumed the air. As long as things were going her way, Ragweed never really needed to sneeze.

Taking the seeds Mom and Pops gave her, Ragweed planted little onions, carrots and tomatoes. She delighted in watching the little seeds sprout. Every day she would run out to see if her garden had flourished. And Carl could barely keep himself contained as he would leer over at Ragweed's little garden, with his mower at full throttle, and scowl. "Too bad", thought Ragweed. "Scowl away."

Once Ragweed's "garden plot" began to take shape, the grass surrounding it looked even more disgusting, and another "plot" began to form. Strolling along the edge of the lawn, Ragweed contemplated on just how to change a bigger part of the landscape, without anyone knowing how it happened. But how? She thought about an overnight planting of Elephant Ear with its giant leaves. "It might be a little hard to sneak those past Carl," chuckled Ragweed. Plus it would be a huge amount of work, which Ragweed really was allergic to. Then, all of a sudden, she remembered her beanbag toys, and a smile began to lighten up her face.

The ever-resourceful Ragweed would plant her own beans. She would miss her two beanbag toys, but those beans would do the trick. They would get watered; they would grow; they would annoy. With her "plot" hatched, Ragweed crept inside, and grabbed the beanbag toys. She then meticulously cut a hole in each bag, just big enough to let a few beans out at a time, and then snuck back outside, strolling casually across the grass; going about the entire yard, planting "bean" seeds everywhere. To tell the truth, Ragweed was more than a little amazed at how many beans it took to put a toy together. Then Ragweed sat back and waited.

With all the water and fertilizer, it didn't take long for little bean plants to sprout; all over the place; in no certain order. Up they came. Much to Ragweed's delight, Carl, the gardener, was mystified on a weekly basis with the sprouting of these little plants. Every week he would come, more would be sprouting up out of that highly manicured grass, in different spots than the week before. He mumbled things like. "What on earth are these? I don't understand what is going on. I used the same grass seed. Where did these things come from? And why are they ruining my-

Adventures with Ragweed

lawn?"

Just when Carl thought he had gotten them all, more would pop up in defiance. He apologized many times over to Moms and Pops, who thought Carl had probably been tipping a bit of the "sauce", and should spend more time paying attention to their lawn.

Ragweed just watched and smiled as a symphony of Mother Nature's making was played out on the lawn. For a short period of time, the lawn had become a wild place where anything could happen and it was fun to watch. Finally the seeds quit sprouting up, but Ragweed didn't care. And even when there were no more sprouts, Carl continued to come out each week with a giant vat of poison, just in case a sprout would rear its ugly head. He was crazed over his lack of lawn control. It was great. He would never be the same.

Ragweed never told anyone what she had done, and never would. It was a delicious memory; a mystery that only she would know about. And whenever Moms would bring up the odd little plants that sprung up from nowhere, Ragweed would smile. And Carl would get a crazed look on his face, and go home early.

And, best of all, Ragweed had learned a lesson. She realized she could now look at any lawn and even grass could always be just one step away from a garden.

It was hot, hot, hot. Too hot to be outdoors, or even indoors Ragweed was thinking. Moms and Pops had come up with the grand idea of a desert adventure. This adventure consisted of a summer trip to Palm Desert, staying in an exclusive hotel, visiting the spa, golfing (if you were crazy enough), getting a face lift (if you needed one), and other stuff Ragweed had no interest in.

Ragweed had talked her (only) friend Marney into coming with them to Palm Desert in the summer, saying it would be loads of fun, and other stuff that Marney always fell for when Ragweed talked her into doing things. And there was really nothing much to do when they got there, except sweat.

So Ragweed wracked her brain to come up with an appropriate adventure. She sipped her lemonade and stared out the window at the heat waves and thought "Yukk." "At least they didn't plan on going to Death Valley this time of year, " piped in Marney. "I read where it's 126 degrees out there." 115 degrees in Palm Desert wasn't exactly frigid to Ragweed. There must be something to do in this heat.

And then, all of a sudden, Ragweed got that look in her eye. Marney always got worried when Ragweed got inspired. "We shall perform a scientific experiment," declared Ragweed. "We shall see if you can actually fry an egg on the sidewalk."

"What?" asked Marney.

People here are always saying "It's so hot you could fry an egg on the sidewalk. I think we need to find out if that is actually possible".

"I don't think so," said Marney. "I think we should go to the pool."

But Ragweed was already off on her new idea. So Marney, as usual, was out of luck.

There was plenty of sidewalk at their swanky hotel, a grill in the making. But where would they get eggs? Ragweed already had that figured out. She went to the kitchen and said she needed three eggs ("Three eggs," thought Marney, "Oh dear.") in their shells for Ragweed's morning facial. Marney almost groaned out load. What a load of hooey. The only thing Ragweed ever did, besides trying to control her hair, was take a shower and be done with it all. A facial, Marney did not think so.

Ragweed also managed to talk to the kitchen and get a spatula, a spoon and a couple plates. It seems that people that stay at swanky hotels are never asked "Why." They just do weird stuff and it's expected. And Ragweed's hair, which had taken on the look of a corn stalk that day, was never even looked at twice by the employees. Who knew, maybe eggs could finally tame Ragweed's hair? Of course Ragweed realized that might be too gross of a solution for her runaway locks, even for her to consider.

With three eggs raw in their shells, a spoon, spatula and a plate, Ragweed and Marney went down to their favorite part of the sidewalk, the part in front of the entrance to the hotel, right in front of the fake falls.

Of course, Ragweed, to that point, had never cooked a single thing. She boiled water once, but certainly that had nothing to do with frying eggs. Even Ragweed knew that much. Marney, who often gave sensible advice to Ragweed, did know how to cook. So, Marney talked Ragweed through frying eggs on the sidewalk. "First you crack the eggs carefully, don't let the shells get in them, don't put them too close together," and that sort of advice. And those eggs began to sizzle to Ragweed's utter delight. They were going to actually perform a scientific experiment. She would have to tell the girls at her elite private school all about this. Too bad she didn't talk the kitchen out of some salt and pepper.

The eggs surely did cook. They sizzled away. And then they looked done. So Ragweed grabbed the spatula, and went to get them up off the sidewalk, to put them on the plate. Unfortunately, those eggs did not budge. They were embedded in that concrete. It was a sticky, gooey mess, and fairly gross looking. It was, basi-

cally, disgusting. Ragweed had in the course of an hour performed a disgusting scientific experiment, and ruined the entrance to the hotel forever. "Not bad for a days work," thought Ragweed.

Other guests' vehicles came and went during all this. But no one had paid the two girls frying eggs on the sidewalk at the entrance any specific attention. And for that they were very grateful. They knew that Moms and Pops were due to leave the hotel for a meeting at any minute. Which meant that Moms and Pops would soon drive by the egg difficulty. And they would notice.

So Ragweed and Marney got busy sloshing the water from the fake falls on to the sidewalk to clean up the mess. They were totally

drenched by the time they were done. And the egg was diminished, but not entirely gone.

And Ragweed and Marney boogied back to their rooms.

Apparently the incident is part of the hotel folklore today. "Here is where two crazy idiots tried to fry eggs on the sidewalk in the middle of summer." That sort of thing. This was not exactly as Ragweed wanted to be remembered. But the good news was that neither Moms nor Pops ever suspected Ragweed of that debacle, "Ragweed cooking? I don't think so," said Moms.

After that day, Ragweed never ate another fried egg. Too many memories….

Linda Lou Crosby

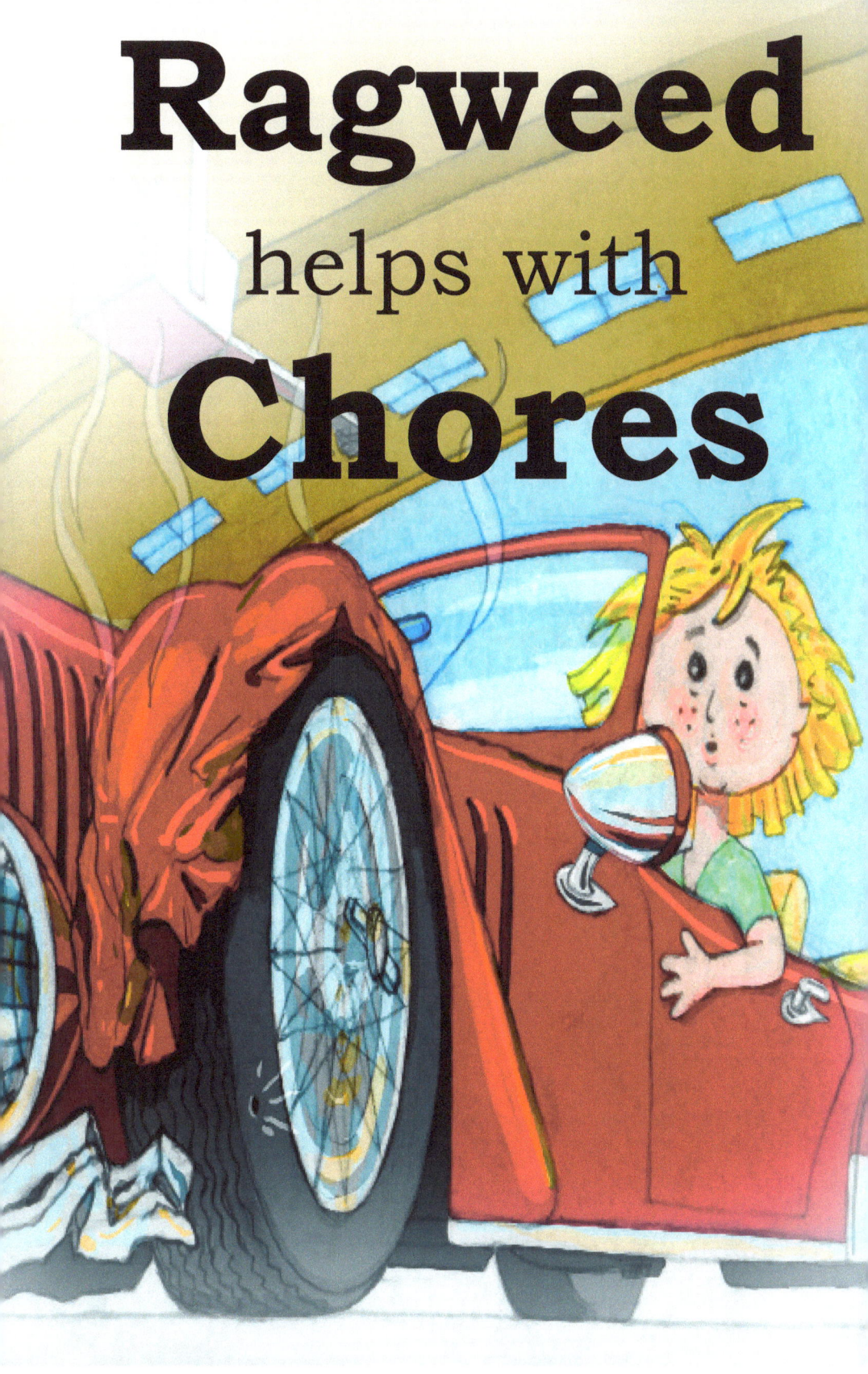

Ragweed's parents were rich; very, very rich. She lacked for nothing, except for something to actually do. Well, besides play tennis, that is. So, one day for no reason that anyone could figure out as they looked back on what was now referred to as "That Fateful Day", Ragweed decided to do "things" around the house. It turned out to be a day Ragweed did things "to" the house, but that was certainly not her original plan.

Ragweed was bored. That's how it all began. Why her Moms and Pops never caught on that boredom was at the bottom of all the various catastrophes connected to Ragweed, she never knew. And she also didn't care. Ragweed only knew that it was time for action of some sort. And today Ragweed decided to be helpful, which should have sent a warning signal out to everyone at her over sumptuous estate....if they only had been paying attention. But no one was in tune...Not Carl the gardener, not Edwina the cook, and certainly not Moms and Pops, which caused Ragweed to smile as she began her day.

First she pasted back her hair with some sort of hair glop Moms had found. Moms was ever hopeful that Ragweed's hair would one day stay in place....so Moms had tried everything from hair paste, to hair spray, to roll on glue (water soluble, of course) to tame Ragweed's unruly locks. It mattered not. Ragweed would start off the day looking perfectly coiffed and be mistaken for a Brussels sprout within two hours. Hence the name Ragweed.

On this most interesting day in Ragweed's history, she dreamed a romantic notion of vacuuming, and dusting, and maybe even ironing. Ragweed's best friend Marney, who was normally dragged along on any escapade (frequently against her wishes), knew that Ragweed had finally completely and utterly lost her mind. Marney hated chores. Taking out the trash...not too much fun. And it smelled bad. But no matter what Marney said to Ragweed that day, Ragweed heard not a single word. And off Ragweed went to be of assistance.

Her first attempt at usefulness was actually pretty cool. Ragweed offered to help Pops park the family's new convertible into the garage. Pops NEVER let anyone drive his favorite cars. And that red Bugati convertible was high on the list. Sure chauffeur's drove the big Rolls Royce to deliver Ragweed around town, but that was different. This was a collectable convertible. And it was almost sacred in Pops' eyes.

Pops should have had warning bells going off in his brain, really loud warning bells, when Ragweed asked to help park Pops' car. First of all, Ragweed never drove anything, anywhere, at any time. She was always chauffeured. Why Pops thought Ragweed knew how to drive continues to be a mystery even today. But it was the one idea Ragweed had for "chores" that Marney thought would be fun, so Marney immediately jumped into the passenger side of the shiny red convertible to ride along. Dad, feeling delighted that his daughter had an interest in something other than herself, went back into the house smiling.

It took Ragweed some fumbling around to find out how to start the car. Marney was quite helpful, as Marney's dad had given her several driving lessons in the fairgrounds parking lot. And everything seemed pretty simple…..push the accelerator, steer carefully around into the garage, don't go too fast, and then turn off the key. Ragweed went carefully forward.

At just that moment, Moms peered outside from the third floor window, and was momentarily speechless. After Moms got her bearings, she yelled "STOP!" from her perch. But with the car motor going, and the window being closed, Ragweed could not make out what Moms said; so she just waved back at Moms and continued on. Unfortunately when Ragweed took her eye off the garage to wave at Moms, things began a downward spiral. Marney realized the error almost immediately and tried to grab the steering wheel to avoid a mishap. But Ragweed would have none of that. It was her day to park the car. So she grabbed the steering wheel back, which only added to the problem. To sum it all up, Ragweed did park the car - right into the corner of the garage. CRUNCH.

Linda Lou Crosby

Silence reined for what seemed like an eternity to everyone, except Pops who had no idea about what had just happened to his Bugati. The best thing that can be said about Ragweed's driving that day was at least she had the good sense not to backup. Marney could not get out of her door, of course, as it was dented in, so she scrambled over Ragweed, and raced for home.

In fact, although Ragweed insisted that Marney was partly to blame for the whole affair, since no one had actually seen Marney in the car except Ragweed, Marney was never held accountable for the unfortunate incident. And Ragweed was grounded – for

the rest of her life – and beyond. She would never have any allowance again, and she would have to get a job at MacDonald's. And that was only the beginning of what Pops decreed after he discovered the mess.

It was anything but an auspicious beginning for Ragweed doing "chores". She felt pretty low, but thought that if she was actually helpful, Pops might even like her again, someday. So Ragweed got idea number two, which ended up not much better than her first idea. But who knew? Ragweed always had a certain logic she went by. No one in the entire universe would ever understand

that logic, but Ragweed did, and that is what mattered.

Ragweed figured if she had to get a job at MacDonald's she had better get familiar with food service. And off she went to the kitchen. She explained to the kitchen help that it was essential that she learn about kitchen activities, so she would be helping them for the day. Looks were exchanged. Eyes were rolled. But Ragweed was the boss's daughter, so "Oh well." And they let her do things in the kitchen.

The family had eaten artichokes for lunch, and the leaves were gathered in plates on the sink. So Ragweed gathered all the leaves, stuffed them into the garbage disposal, and turned it on. The three cooks turned around in unison with a most astonished look on their face. Ragweed had a huge smile on hers as the garbage disposal, which was the most advanced, expensive garbage disposal in the known universe, gradually ground to a halt. The kitchen help tried every thing to pry the stringy mess loose, but nothing worked. Unfortunately Pops walked in during this strange event, and basically went ballistic, which was a real change in his personality. Ragweed was now grounded for two lifetimes, would eat all her food in her room from now on, and was not allowed to use the phone for a year.

Uh oh. This was getting serious. When Pops stormed out of the kitchen, he was muttering incoherent things. And Ragweed just stood there dumbfounded while the kitchen help went to find the plumber's number. Ragweed realized that things were a bit urgent as a party of 20 had been invited to dinner, and things weren't looking real good right then. The kitchen folks had been getting ready to do the dishes when the chokes hit the fan, and the dishes were piled pretty high.

Ragweed felt so bad, she decided to do something she said she never, ever would do, and started rinsing dishes (in the back bathroom – as the kitchen sink was inoperable at the time), and putting them in the dishwasher. She actually did a half decent job of getting the dishes ready (amazingly enough), and then Ragweed went looking for dish soap. Ragweed knew that if she could bring about a clean kitchen Pops would realize her heart was in the right place, even if a few things hadn't gone well. She knew all would be forgiven, and she could once again use her phone.

She actually turned out to predict a correct ending to this difficult day, but not for the reasons she thought. Ragweed slowly measured the soap into the dishwasher and figured out how to put it on the correct cycle, and pushed start. Finally, something was working the way it was supposed to. Ragweed was saved. She went off to get her Moms and Pops to celebrate victory.

As the three approached the kitchen they were completely amazed. Apparently Ragweed had mistakenly put clothes washing soap into the dishwasher, so bubbly suds were waist high over the entire kitchen, and oozing on into the living room.

Panic set in for Ragweed as she knew she would now be banished to somewhere in Siberia, where she would freeze to death, without a phone. Instead something very different happened. Pops turned to Ragweed and although he was red as a beet and smoke was coming out of his ears, he took a deep breath and calmly said, "I give up. Ragweed you could never, ever pay us back with your time or allowance or phone minutes for the damages you have caused today. So forget the penalties I gave you, forget my taking away your allowance, forget being prohibited from using your phone, forget being banished to your room. I just want you to promise me one thing." Ragweed waited …. "I want you to promise me and your Moms and all those who work with us and for us at our home that you will NEVER, EVER, EVER help with any housework again."

So Ragweed quickly shot out of the kitchen, and went back to her room, and never, ever even considered doing a chore ever again.

Ragweed sat on the ground and let the Sycamore's falling leaves shower her with golden yellow, orange and red. Fall was her favorite time of year: pumpkin patches, apple trees and the crisp air proclaiming Halloween was not far away.

"Get packed. We are going to Mexico." Ragweed was still daydreaming when her mother shouted this message from the back door several feet away.

"Mexico?" thought Ragweed, "Why Mexico?"

"We are going to Mexico to make a travel fishing show. And Pops is going to be the producer," Moms announced as Ragweed walked through the door.

Ragweed couldn't ever remember the family going fishing. She wasn't even sure if her extravagantly wealthy Pops would dare touch a worm. Didn't you have to stick your hand underneath dirt, germs and other ungodly things like GRIME? Pops country club status would come to a halt if word got out, Ragweed was sure of that.

Moms must have ESP. She was conversing with Ragweed who hadn't yet said a word out loud.

"We are going to La Paz, and rent a fishing boat, and travel by regular plane – like regular people."

"We are not regular people," Ragweed mused to herself. *"In fact, I have no idea what kind of people we really are, but certainly not regular."*

"And Pops is going to film it all," continued Moms. "And we will have the Rolls Royce shipped to La Paz by boat."

Ragweed was really concerned at this point. The Rolls wasn't exactly what she thought a fishing car would look like. And who would want to watch a weird family driving around La Paz in a

Rolls Royce after a day of fishing?

Pops was an idea man and when his "light bulb" went off there was no stopping him. Once Pops had developed a sure fire way to keep dogs in the back seat of a car. Pops called it his "Doggie Stay Put" device. It was a hand with a finger pointing to the back seat, and every time it went up and down it would say "Stay." The most notice ever paid to the darn thing was when Pop's Irish Wolfhound, Herman, landed in the back seat of the Rolls, and promptly ate the hand - ending THAT project.

And then there was the "pre-knotted" string tie. There was a slight flaw: Once you snapped them on, they wouldn't come off. Needless to say, there were a lot of unhappy customers.

Yet, one day the family was rich.

Whatever idea Pops sold that had made him wealthy, no one could remember. Pops couldn't even remember. Ragweed was certain it was an accident, albeit a very wealthy one. Pops was considered handsome, so he did commercials now and then, and dabbled in voice overs. So it's possible he stumbled into something.

But this new idea of a fishing show, well, thinking of Pops as a producer was unsettling.

For one, he was extremely disorganized. And Moms added to the fray by being forever excited by Pops newest idea. Why Moms had even made a special store display for the "Doggie Stay Put" device, and gone to a department store as a "demo lady", properly disguised of course. Her "I Love Lucy" look had not captivated crowds. And Moms was on to the next "big idea" the following day. Now Moms was focused on Mexico.

Ragweed was leery of the idea.

But, if the whole family was in the mix, the outcome was inevitable. They were going to Mexico. As Moms went on and on, casting phrases, like "Buenos Dias" and "Adios" as she spoke, Ragweed had a sort of vacant smile on her face. Ragweed knew there was no changing the direction of this looming catastrophe. Still, Ragweed couldn't bring herself to actually move or to say a word.

"So, what are you waiting for?" asked Moms. "Get packed." And she whisked off down the hall.

"What does one pack for fishing?" thought Ragweed. *"Hooks, worms, maybe a net….. and would any of it fit in a suitcase? Mexico? What to wear – when in doubt, don't leave it out!"*

Ragweed found a trunk, and began throwing whatever clothes she could find in it. Multiple shirts, shorts, formals, underwear, hats, and whatever else she could grab went into that trunk. How Ragweed even found her clothes was remarkable as her bedroom was classified as one of the major wonders of the world to both she and her Moms.

No matter how neat Ragweed tried to keep her room, things were always popping out of drawers and closets. Sort of like her hairdo, which was tied into a ponytail first thing each morning but

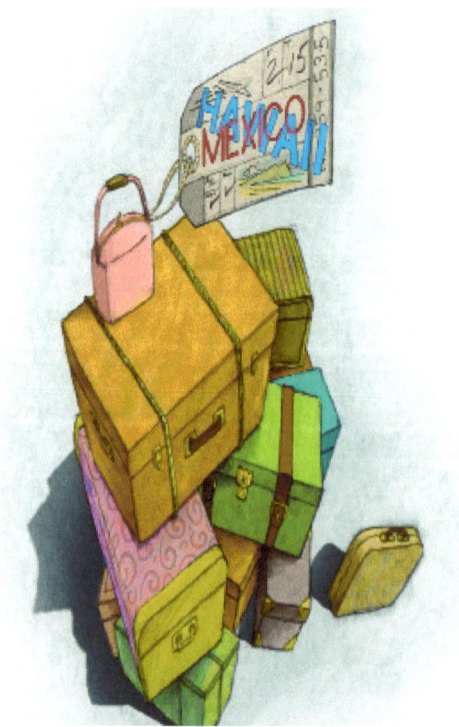

by dinnertime became like a thatched roof. Hence, another reason for her name: Ragweed.

When Moms had said they were traveling like regular people, Ragweed didn't realize she meant no private jet. That meant no chauffeur to *lug* the baggage and no one to deposit her at the airfield. From the look of the stacked trunks, suitcases and sundry bags stacked in the hall, Ragweed thought the trip to the airport was going to be an adventure in itself.

Ragweed would need some backup.

Having only one real friend narrowed the companion options – Marney it would be.

"But Moms and Pops," it's important for me to have a friend along in a strange country," Ragweed pleaded. "Marney even speaks Spanish."

"Really," Moms raised an eyebrow, "I thought Marney was from an Indian village in Alaska?"

Eventually Ragweed wore her parents down and they agreed to let "bilingual" Marney from Alaska join them.

****

It would be a pilot for a weekly fishing show, Pops told Moms on the drive to the airport as he threw out titles he had conceived earlier that day.

"'Traveling with Moms and Pops', catchy name isn't it," Pops beamed smiling ear to ear.

"Isn't it exciting," Moms said turning toward the girls sitting between the trunks in the backseat.

Pops got the producer/director job for the show when the initial selectee got sick. Since it was Pops first crack behind the camera, he thought it best to pick people already in the business.

An audio guy Pops had worked with on prior projects, Sherm, became the acting director.

Ragweed had her doubts.

"He'll be great Pops. After all, he's known for his audio work on a puppet show on our local T.V. station" Moms, using her telepathy powers yet again, announced. Hank the cameraman was joining Pops crew too. Hank was from another weekly show called "Cooking with Cora" – where the title took on an entirely different meaning altogether – as Cora and Hank dipped into the cooking Sherry and White Wine as well as … well you get the picture.

Bub also joined the team.

"I didn't know he was in the business," Moms said.

"He likes to fish," quipped Pops.

"Well it is a fishing show," Marney chimed.

***

The ticket agent assured Pops all their bags could be sent under one ticket to make claiming them in Mexico easier. While Pops was finalizing the baggage plans, Ragweed noticed an airline worker near the family trunks.

He was ticketing the baggage for Hawaii!

"Pops," Ragweed tugged on his arm.

"Not now Ragweed," said Pops.

"But, Pops, our bags…" said Ragweed, a bit louder.

"I am taking care of the bags," said Pops a little bit louder.

"But Pops, we have a problem…"

"I said NOT NOW," yelled Pops with a finality that stopped further discussion.

So Ragweed watched as 17 trunks and bags, well 18 if you counted Marney's, headed to what looked like Hawaii.

***

Everyone climbed on the flight, regular class, as they were traveling like regular people, and flew to Mexico.

Ragweed was delighted that it was just a quick change of planes to head to La Paz, with a minimal stop at customs.

"Nothing much to declare," said Pops.

"Little does he know how right he is," Ragweed mused to herself.

***

The flight into Mexico was uneventful and when the family landed, their car and the film crew was there to greet them at La Paz. However, there was something missing …

"Where's our luggage?" Pops quizzed the puzzled airport crew.

"How many bags are we talking?" asked a clerk.

There were 17 trunks, 18 if you counted Marney's.

"I know where our bags are," Ragweed piped up.

"Where," asked Pops, looking incredulous and harassed at the same time.

"The bags went to Hawaii," said Ragweed, "That's what I was trying to tell you at the airport in L.A."

Before Pops could say another word, a gentleman came up with a rather ordinary brown suitcase, and said "Mr. Latimer…we have your suitcase."

"I am NOT Mr. Latimer," said Pops.

Turns out that Mr. Latimer's suitcase had gone to Mexico, while Mr. Latimer had gone to Hawaii. And Mr. Latimer was probably quite dumbfounded to learn he was the proud recipient of 17 trunks, (18 if you counted Marney's).

It would be two to three days before the luggage made its way back to Ragweed and family. In the meantime, everyone went shopping to get the basics. Along with shirts, shorts and undergarments, Moms made sure to buy some extra hair gel to try and control Ragweed's unruly hair. It would not look good on camera sticking out everywhere. Meanwhile, the crew was busy connecting with a regular fishing ship, and figuring out where to store their equipment, and where they could setup for various scenes, and so on.

***

Fishing day would have the crew filming on a boat with a captain, an outrigger, a toilet and some seats. The crew wanted to take it for a spin to see how the setup would work.

Never having been on a fishing trip, Moms wanted to ensure the family packed properly for the outing: Lunch, rubber bands, extra shoes, hats and drinks. The family left early wanting to get a good start.

Captain Miguel, however, had already come and gone. Apparently his definition of "early" was different than Moms and Pops. Unfortunately, Miguel had shown up before the sun came up, so by the time Ragweed and her family made their way to the dock, it was too late, which was just fine with Ragweed.

Enter Day Two.

Ah, the open sea and fresh air. Pops stayed optimistic. But as the boat chugged into the open water, the ride became choppy and the ocean waves got bigger. Up. Down. Up. Down. Swish to one side. Swish to another side. Up. Down. The vessel swayed.

The camera and audio guy - also the director - were puking into the water over the side of the boat.

Pops was undeterred insisting the show must go on. The footage was extraordinary – Ragweed had never seen so many sick people or heard such accurate sound effects.

"Maybe they're filming a horror show," Marney offered. That's what Ragweed loved best about her friend, Marney, she was a forward thinker.

Eventually the weather got better and the crew was able to film the trip even capturing some great Marlin fishing shots. It turns out the final product, with the "live weather report," "ghastly sound effects," and a few "four letter words," wasn't what the television executives had in mind. Overall, when said and done, this time Pops "great" idea only put him $100,000 in the hole.

The trip home was quiet. Even the luggage managed to follow the family properly. But Pops did make a declaration once they landed in L.A. – no more fishing. After several showers, he could still smell the salt water and Marlin skin. He decided right then, he would never make a film again – of any kind. For that Ragweed was grateful.

A little horse manure, a bit of kitchen vegetable scraps, some newspapers and Ragweed was on to her new adventure, saving the planet by making compost. As Marney (Ragweed's only friend) helped Ragweed gather the various things needed for compost, she knew they both were doomed. Compost, has been defined in the Free Online dictionary as "A mixture of decaying organic matter, as from leaves and manure, used to improve soil structure and provide nutrients." You were supposed to build it beginning slowly, with a small number of layers. The pile would heat up in due time and then you would add more, and so it should go. And then you added it to your plants, instead of commercial fertilizer. Sounded easy enough.

Making compost a la Ragweed not only would become a monumental messy failure, but it would smell really bad. That was because Ragweed had skipped the basics and gone straight for building the pile, which became a tall steaming mass of frightening proportions, with a LOT of manure…that fact was quite obvious.

In fact, as the pile of various ingredients grew her family's opulent estate was looking less like "Better Homes and Gardens" and more like the county dump.

These insignificant issues mattered not to Ragweed. She was determined that her family's most extravagant lifestyle would change. Moms and Pops would become more self sufficient, live off the land, go green, get off the grid, cook with solar ovens, hitchhike to vacation spots, you name it. And the first task was to learn to make compost.

Ragweed had recently read that one of the most important reasons to compost is to save money on fertilizer. She knew that Pops would welcome that notion. The fact that the family could also could help reduce environmental issues only added to (what Ragweed imagined) was the "green" appeal. Of course, when you consider that the gigantic mound of newspapers, horse manure, kitchen scraps, cardboard boxes, sawdust, nutshells, and heaven knows what else that Ragweed had coaxed the help at her estate and Marney to collect and pile was uncontained and basically out of control, perhaps Ragweed had missed a few steps along the way.

Ragweed wanted to get the thing in place before Moms and Pops returned from their Hawaiian vacation….as a big surprise. She certainly met the mark on that point.

Their immediate neighbor, the grumpy Mrs. Cruikshank, had begun to refer to their place as Mount Trashdump. And as Moms and Pops were returning home from their Hawaiian vacation, they noticed a certain smell (a cross between a meat packing plant and a septic tank) that completely mystified them, coming from the direction of their estate. Unfortunately the mystery was solved as they pulled up to their gate, and observed a ten-foot high mountain of indescribable organic mass. Moms fainted on the spot, and Pops went ballistic. It was not the reaction Ragweed was hoping for.

Many of the cypress trees that lined the entrance were also lined with newspaper. That had happened because Ragweed insisted on piling newspapers on the giant mess without wetting

them down. A swift wind would come along and spiral the classifieds over every estate within 5 miles. If you missed the morning paper and wanted the front page, you had to start at Mrs. Cruikshank's, and then go for the business section at Tex Holland's, and so on. Mrs. Cruikshank was under psychiatric care, and unknowingly, Moms and Pops were just about under indictment for distributing newspapers without a license. Things were not ideal, to say the least.

During Moms and Pops absence, Carl the gardener had put in a letter of resignation, which Ragweed had promptly added to the pile. So it had not yet become official. The help were wearing gas masks. And even Ragweed began to have her doubts.

Pops was way beyond asking "Why me?" He already knew there was no answer for that. But in Pops' wildest dreams he could NOT imagine even Ragweed would come up with such a nincompoop of an idea. Ragweed started giving Pops her spiel about ecological behavior and the like, and when she got to the part about being able to use the methane gas that was created by the compost pile to power the Bugati, Pops flipped his lid.

Adventures with Ragweed

At the precise moment when Ragweed's existence looked to be in peril, who should show up but former rodeo clown and neighboring millionaire Tex Holland. Tex loved a good challenge. And this was better than most. In fact, Tex looked to Ragweed to come up with problems that only he could solve. Being from Texas, where everything is done on a huge scale, the compost pile looked about the right size to Tex. He was always saying, "You think that's big, you should see what we have in Texas." But he never said that about the compost pile that he proposed to move to his place, so he could plant "the biggest apple trees around" (heck, the pile could have a couple of apple trees hidden in it already thought Tex) and insisted on paying for it with cash. "Paying for it?" thought Pops. "Rodeo clowns are crazier than I thought."

Ragweed was a bit disappointed that her idea had basically changed direction. But when Spring came the following year, Tex invited Ragweed to come see the apples on his tree. Ragweed would never call New York, 'The Big Apple' again. Why Tex's apples were bigger than cannonballs….. It took an axe to cut them off the tree, so they say.

Ragweed mows the Lawn

Ragweed was sitting in her room after days of rain. Although there was usually something to keep her occupied, Ragweed was running out of stuff to do. This always signaled difficulties for others who knew her. But no one had ever learned to read the signs of boredom, so it was their fault if they were unprepared for the approaching scenario.

Ragweed and her Moms and Pops lived in an extravagantly lavish home in Montecito. They had oodles of money, a mega landscape around their place, people who worked for them to take care of things, and lots of big toys. At least that is what Ragweed thought they were. To her a red Bugati convertible was a "toy", to Pops it was an essential conveyance to get places in. And so it went. Moms and Pops were entirely too busy, doing whatever, to keep track of Ragweed, and that is exactly how she liked it.

Ragweed's one and only friend, Marney, lived some miles away. So, needing someone to do something with, Ragweed called Marney to come over that day, and sent their Rolls to pick her up. Marney said she would rather walk, and did, waving at the Rolls as it passed by on its way to Marney's house. Marney arrived refreshed, although never quite prepared for what Ragweed might think of next. And this day was no exception.

Today Ragweed wanted to be outdoors. And she had a plan that would make outdoors more interesting. This plan included hotwiring the riding mower, and taking a tour of the ten-acre estate she lived on. Marney's eyes grew wide with concern. "What about Carl, the gardener?" Marney asked.

"It is Saturday", Ragweed replied, "Carl is not here. And nobody else ever goes into the work shed but Carl." The work shed was a 50x70 beautifully appointed building, with ornate doors, that housed all the basic equipment used on the estate. "And we are going mower riding," said Ragweed emphatically.

Marney, for some reason, had never been able to say "No!" to Ragweed, and she didn't change her pattern on that day either. So, with considerable foreboding, and some excitement, Marney accompanied Ragweed on a "sneak" up to the "shed", looking for the riding mower.

The riding mower was a top of the line John Deere ZTrak Z900 R Series, with Comfort and Convenience controls, the Hydraulic Cross-Porting System, the Brake-N-Go foot pedal start, and a 3-year, 1500 hour warranty……which turned out to be a good thing, and very useful after the events that would soon transpire.

Although it only had one seat, the mower seat was big enough for both Marney and Ragweed to squeeze aboard. Pundits say that starting a riding lawn mower can take some time when the engine is cold. Starting when the engine is cold will require extra cranking time to move the fuel from the fuel tank to the engine. BUT do not allow the starter to crank for more than 15 seconds at a time. Ragweed read the instructions,….somewhat. Stage one of this looming disaster. Ragweed read that she was supposed to sit in the seat and press the clutch/brake lever on the left side of the mower with her left foot…and be sure to set the parking brake with the knob or lever on the right side of the mower……unfortunately, she performed the first task but ignored the parking brake. Soon to be a big mistake.

Ragweed actually figured out the choke (with Marney's help), cranked it for two long, flooded it, had to wait, and finally the darn thing started. Ragweed also put the "go" lever into the "rabbit" position (read FAST), and by accident engaged the drive and mower attachments, and off they went. It was surprising to both Ragweed and Marney at how fast a mower could actually go. And, by the way, they did not know how to stop it, or slow it down.

One could only hope this story would have some sort of magical ending, but it doesn't. Not only did Ragweed mow through everything on her way to the edge of the property, she wasn't very good at steering. So the darn thing careened about at top speed mowing everything in its path. And then they went on to the neighbor's estate, the grumpy Mrs. Cruikshank. They crashed through the artfully placed picket fence, mowed the Iris bed down completely, and headed for the rose garden.

Mrs. Cruikshank had heard a strange noise, and came to the patio just in time to see her 50 year old rose garden getting a crew cut. The only thing Ragweed could do, and she could barely do that, was wave, as they headed for "Tex" Loveland's grand manor. Somehow, "Tex" who was obviously from Texas, had bought 50 acres when he retired as a rodeo clown, and even had horses on the place. Tex was always up for a challenge, and saw just the thing coming his way.

Ragweed had finished off Mrs. Cruikshank's bromeliad's on her way out and smashed through Tex's split rail fencing without a backward glance. At that point both Ragweed and Marney were looking for an immediate exit from the mower, and were hoping for a soft place to land. As they and the mower approached a pile of hay, Tex had gone to grab his rope, built a lasso, and was heading in their direction. In a ballet-like feat of perfection, both girls bailed off the mower into the hay, just as Tex lassoed the mower, bulldogged it to the ground, and shut it off in one masterful stroke.

While Mrs. Cruikshank was busy calling her lawyer to sue

Adventures with Ragweed

Moms and Pops within an inch of their full bank account, Tex told the girls he hadn't had so much fun in 20 years, since he retired from the rodeo circuit. The girls were welcome on his place anytime. And then Tex hitched the mower to the back of his pickup, while the girls rode in his special bucket seats inside, and home Ragweed went.

The reaction with Moms and Pops was mixed. Pops was delighted and amazed that Ragweed had managed to run the mower, quite a technical achievement, while Moms was really mad. She had tea with Mrs. Cruikshank once a week, and still worries to this day that Mrs. Cruikshank might lace her tea with something unpleasant.

The damage was eventually fixed. Pops and Tex became friends, which lead to some other interesting eventualities. And Ragweed and Marney learned to ride horses at Tex's place.

Is there a moral to this story? I don't think so. But it sure sounds like it was a fun day to me.

Ragweed builds a Float

It had been a busy year for Ragweed. That very fact made it REALLY busy for her friends and her Moms and Pops. Anything that Ragweed decided to do invariably included many people who had no idea they would soon be caught up in something unusual, irritating, and sometimes quite infuriating. This year would be no exception.

It was actually towards the end of the year, and Ragweed decided that she and her friends were going to build a float for the yearly Christmas Parade. Ragweed actually had only one friend, Marney, but Ragweed had a plan that would include all the girls at her school as well. They just didn't know it yet.

The theme of this year's parade was "Hidden Treasures". The theme got Ragweed to thinking; a problem for all who would soon be involved in one of the most monumental, time consuming, resource overloaded, irritating events ever.

Ragweed had been studying Latin at the Mayberry Girls High School. One of her projects (which was actually not requested by the teacher, as you can well imagine) was to translate a version of Winnie the Poo into Latin, and have a reader's theater during "Play Week" at her school. It turned out to be pretty strange for the audience watching five girls dressed up as Winnie the Poo characters, speaking Latin poorly (the one playing Eeyore got an award for worst actor ever in a school play), for a fifteen-minute play. The characters were all laughing hysterically at their lines, while the audience was basically dumbfounded. Ragweed's drama teacher was not amused.

Through Ragweed's interest in Latin, she came across the story of the Trojan Horse. Basically the Greeks had put one over on the Romans by giving them the gift of a humongous Trojan horse statue, which had lots of Greek warriors hidden inside. Not exactly "Hidden Treasures" for the Romans, but the idea was a sure winner for a float. Ragweed just knew it. Marney just knew that Ragweed was nuts, and vowed to have absolutely nothing to do with this crazy idea. And so Marney was extremely surprised to find herself calling all the girls at school telling them what a cool idea Ragweed had for a float.

As always with Ragweed's ideas, the upcoming event or adventure was only days away, so everyone had to work at a feverish pitch to get "it" done. And this would follow right along in that vein.

There were planning meetings at school…..somehow this had become the school entry for the Christmas Parade….and planning and working meetings after school. Brothers and fathers were enlisted. The Trojan horse float would be 14 feet tall, and roll along being towed by Tex Holland's pickup truck (Tex, one of Ragweed's neighbors, was a former cowboy rodeo clown with zillions of dollars. And he was the only one who dared to have a pickup truck in the opulent Montecito estates). Purposefully not letting Moms or Pops in on the plan, the float "team" began gathering lumber and wheels, and stuff to cover the float at Ragweed's estate. Moms and Pops had been away on a little trip to the Norton Simon museum in Pasadena, and were beyond amazed as they arrived home to find a giant wooden horse framed, on wheels, near their garage. Pops could be heard saying something like, "What the #$%^ is that?" And Moms could be heard saying something like, "Now dear, there are children present." Lots and lots of children were present; around a hundred if you counted the Marley twins, who were Marney's five year old sisters, and whom she was officially "babysitting" that day.

Chaos reined. It was a show that the classic comedians like Laurel and Hardy would have been jealous of. Kids were swinging 2x4s around barely missing other kids and Pops' Bugati convertible. Giant rolls of some kind of sheeting were laying about, unfurled at various lengths. Staple guns were rattling off at a tremendous rate.

At one point Marney had stapled Ragweed's hair to the horse's right leg. Although Ragweed was furious, Marney told her it was her own fault for having such a ridiculous scheme. And besides Ragweed's unruly locks were momentarily contained. Ragweed, who started each day looking fairly groomed, had hair that mirrored her personality. It just would expand into all sorts of configurations as the day went on. Today it looked basically like a fright wig.

One of the schoolteachers came to the rescue with Pops…saying soothing things about Latin class, Trojan horses, Christmas Parade Floats…And, "thanks so much for the generous offer of your home". The teacher then ushered Moms and Pops into their kitchen, while the cook prepared tea. Pops decided on something a bit more fortified than tea, and Moms took a nap.

Somehow, a parade float, a weird looking parade float, came to life. It had a bit of a starboard list, which Ragweed explained away as a wound it suffered in the Trojan Wars. *(Say what?)*

In order to move the rolling horse to the parade site, they had to get a special permit from the county, pay the electrical company a small fortune for paving the way with the power lines, and prop up the entire float when they went around corners. And, oh by the way, Pops footed the bill for everything. Somehow Moms hid the various transactions under her petty cash fund, except for the electrical bill for $2,234.93, which stood out like a sore thumb. So Pops went around turning lights off for months afterwards.

As Marney saw it, besides the ridiculous horse itself, there

were two other strange things about the end result. First, the Trojan Horse ended up with a gigantic Christmas ribbon on its nose, which looked bizarre, but kept the whole mess in the spirit of Christmas. And in the middle of the parade little leprechauns (in costumes of course) ran out of the horse, throwing candy to the crowd. Ragweed's school chums were furious about having to dress up as Leprechauns. But when the crowd applauded madly at their antics, they forgave her instantly.

Tex was in his element towing the horsosaurus. He loved a challenge, and this certainly qualified. He even had welded a special hitch to his pickup, and fabricated guy wires to keep the monstrosity from falling over. The float made it to the end of the parade route basically intact, except for a few "shingles" that fell off.

The Float team was given the award known as the "Miracle on 42nd Street" award, which was definitely earned. The school was happy as they had gotten an award; Ragweed was happy as she had seen her float go down the boulevard; Marney was happy that it was all over; and Tex was happy that he actually made it to the dump before the float keeled over, barely missing the dump's gate guard.

Tex continues to wonder to this day why there is a gate guard at the dump. But the answer to that will have to wait for another time.

Ragweed and her Racket

Ragweed chewed on a dandelion stem and pondered her plight as she plopped down on the perfectly manicured grassy hillside. The grass with no blade too tall or too small, sprawled out across the Girls' high school campus. Everything here was *manicured:* dress codes, classes, and *curriculum.*

Everything but Ragweed, of course. Somehow Ragweed's hair, which was very organized in the morning, took on a kind of "weird science" look by noon, and her uniforms, although perfectly ironed to begin with, seemed to crinkle as the day wore on. "How boring," thought Ragweed, as she chewed on a piece of grass and pondered her fate.

And even if she was a former Girls' Invitational Tennis champ, Ragweed felt the tennis gala *had gone a bit wacko.* Ragweed's parents, Moms and Pops, *frequently reminded her,* that it was an honor to be one of three students selected on a scholarship for this private institute of 300. The free ride was due to the school's desire to be recognized for its *tennis* athletics as well as its academic and cultural programs. *It was also about Moms and Pops desire to follow Ragweed around in fuss budget fashion, clucking about tennis matches and results like chickens in a hen house.*

"Whatever," thought Ragweed.

The tennis matches ended up being social *outings* for parents and coaches – *held* for bragging rights of the *"upper crust".* Even the most severe trouncing to a terrible player would give her parents discussion fodder for weeks to follow.

"Irene made me so proud," they would say. "No matter how horrible her forehand was, even when she accidentally hit the line judge in the head, causing a small concussion, she kept a smile on her face. We are so proud."

It was said that an annual Invitational Tournament would give the outings more prestige, *although what exactly was prestigious about* it, Ragweed wasn't sure. Did someone beyond the school actually care?

Did the newspaper even carry the story about a "well fought" "somewhat heated" match when, in desperation, Wiggy had slugged Sad Sally, making her cry for real for once, and got a technical knockout which awarded her a victory? No, you never saw that in the paper.

Ragweed wasn't sure she even wanted to participate, but the more she thought about it: Outwitting her opponents Penelope, the "Lob Queen," Sad Sally, the "crier," and Wiggy with the unmanageable hairdo – all *of a sudden, winning mattered.*

****

It wasn't a bad day for a tournament. The smog was just bad enough so someone could give *terrible line* calls and no one would challenge the decision, *because they couldn't see.* Ragweed had even made the *finals* but no one seemed to notice.

Chatter filled the courtside arena where a tent for afternoon tea was pitched and a band played in the background. To top it off, Penelope was playing on Court 3, and drawing all the attention.

****

It was common practice for players to cheat, feign illness, divert their opponent's attention and do whatever necessary to break the other player's concentration so they could win. *It was the very reason that Ragweed lost during last year's finals. Ragweed had been playing Penelope for hours, and even had a match point, but Penelope's trickery knew no bounds. During an incredible rally, Penelope looked over beyond the crowd, and wailed, "Oh my gosh…oh no…" At which point everybody, including Ragweed, looked over at nothing, of course. That enabled Penelope to drop a short little ball over the net, and win the point.*

Ragweed was so upset that she had been fooled, in such an amateur fashion, that she promptly lost every following point, and the match. But that was last year, and this year would be different for Ragweed. She was convinced.

It didn't help that the Tennis Association had decided against *lending the Girls' Invitational* professional judges, leaving *the* school players to appoint their own referees, which led to some of the shoddiest calls and practices *imaginable. And then there were the parents. Parents who* didn't openly encourage *devious* tactics, behind closed doors applauded their daughter's efforts, *especially* if it meant another notch in Girls' School tennis history.

Ragweed's parents, Moms and Pops, while caught in the world of the privileged, didn't approve of *cheating*. They certainly didn't discourage Ragweed from stalling games, making slow calls on serves, arguing over tennis etiquette and sneezing whenever an opponent tried to hit an overhead – but out and out cheating…that was definitely not allowed.

That's why Ragweed saw nothing ill-willed about sneezing at appropriately tense spots in a match - one of the reasons that Ragweed got her nickname. Everyone assumed Ragweed was aller-

gic, and she was ... to losing points.

Penelope, on the other hand, seemed to have mastered the art of defeating opponents with subtlety so slight that Ragweed thought her more of an actress than tennis player. Even the announcer seemed mesmerized by Penelope.

"Advantage Penelope," the announcement echoed so loudly the band stopped for a moment.

"Good grief," Ragweed mused. "Penelope is still playing."

Not that surprising, however.

Penelope played with a butterfly catcher excuse of a racket and was known as the "Lob Queen." You'd think her 90,000 (or so) lobs that would cross the net would be enough to bore life's most avid supporters. But in spite of the fact that her points took forever, fans weren't deterred from cheering.

Ragweed had her own theories.

Since Penelope played so long, taking time off only for a short lunch and dinner, people had time during her matches to hang out and discuss their finances, luxury vacations and latest new ventures.

It seemed Penelope was good for the economy too.

Any town in which Penelope played brought an immediate increase in business to the local chiropractor. Penelope's opponents always needed some back adjustment, after the match, mind you, and her own family too. It was rumored that Penelope's dad was in a full body cast from watching his daughter's use of the "lob."

There were other tales too of how Penelope's opponents had to hire their own private chiropractors at court sites for obvious neck adjustments during a "heated" competition. The discussion on whether or not such assistance was legal was long ago discarded by Tennis Association Officials themselves. They, after only one set of the great lobber's fluff balls, reaching heights of well over 22 feet at times, decided that in the interest of humane tennis, chiropractors were most definitely allowed.

Apparently while line referees cheered for Penelope, it didn't save them from injury. Linewoman Lottie, after only three games with Penelope, had to quit in the middle of a match because she could no longer look down to accurately call the lines.

Ragweed had to tune out the announcer and forget about Penelope – at least for now. Ragweed had to remain focused. Ragweed had only lost the title once in the past three years and she was determined not to lose it this time – not in her senior year.

Wiggy who was ranked sixth, had never won the tournament and didn't seem to be a threat this year. Players feared her hairdo with cowlicks sticking out from all angles, more than her tennis shots. So frightening was Wiggy's hair that her own mother threatened to cut it using a mower instead of scissors. Of course, it never happened.

Wiggy did almost win a match with chewing gum.

She had spit her gum out at the start of a game and forgot to pick it up when players switched sides. A forehand later and Wiggy's opponent was stuck. The wad was so sticky it delayed the game five minutes while the "surprised" player switched shoes after failing to completely remove the goo. It was the first and last time in the match Wiggy led. Five double faults and Wiggy and her hair were out.

Sad Sally was next.

Drama was her strategy. She'd wail and throw her racket on every point that didn't go her way and if necessary would guilt players into conceding her the game. Ragweed just wore earplugs and tuned her out, an easy win.

"Game, set and match to Penelope," roared the announcer, this alerted Ragweed that only Penelope stood between her and this year's trophy.

****

Tensions were high.

Penelope's parents were more adamant about her need to win than usual.

Ragweed's parents were no better: Pushing, needling, and giving unwanted advice – to the point that Ragweed banned them from being at the tournament.

"I don't want to even see you at the courts!" emphasized Ragweed. And Moms and Pops nodded their heads in agreement, with their fingers crossed behind their backs.

****

Ragweed was tense. She looked serious.

Penelope entered the court. She seemed loose and ready. She even wore a smirk on her face.

Still it would be a good rivalry. Both players wanted to win and surprisingly neither side introduced any questionable tactics. It was pure tennis. Point for point the match went on and on and on and on. One hour, two hours.

Every play became crucial.

Even the crowd, during the intensity of this match was uncharacteristically silenced into attention. It was history in the making. Every parent and player of this class of 1993 knew it would be a day they would never forget.

And then, the unexpected happened.

"Ragweed, watch the ball! What kind of shot was that?"

Then a different lower voice: "Bend your knees, Ragweed!"

It sounded like voices were calling out from the sky.

Ragweed and Penelope looked up at the same time ... that's when a gigantic bird dropping fell into Penelope's path, causing Penelope to skid into the crowd. It wasn't until Penelope toppled into the front row of spectators that she was able to stop. A doctor then leapt from the stands, and determined that Penelope's ankle was too injured to continue play.

Would Penelope actually default? Ragweed didn't want to win like that. Before she or Penelope could react, there was a really loud thud and the distinctive voice of Ragweed's mother screeching, "Help me! Help me!"

All eyes diverted to the tree behind the center stands where a giant tree limb and Pops had crashed to the dirt from nine feet up and Moms was barely hanging on by her fingernails to what was left of the tree branch.

Ragweed's parents had climbed a nearby Sycamore tree and hid in the branches – their idea of conforming to the promise of not being "seen" at the tournament.

The hubbub that followed was intense.

Wiggy's mother thought that her giant purse might help break Moms' fall and Ragweed thought Penelope's butterfly racket could catch Moms. Thankfully the fire truck arrived in time to avert all plans.

After Moms was rescued by a few fascinated firefighters and Pops was taken to the hospital from his mishap with the Sycamore tree, it was decided Ragweed would indeed win by default.

"Default, then what was the point?" Ragweed fumed.

No really, what was the point count when the match had been halted? No one could remember since the scoreboard had been run over and shredded by the rescuing fire truck. So, not only did Ragweed win by a technicality, it was the only time in the history of the Girls School Championship that there was no score.

And for once, no one cared!!!!!

It's not that easy being green'. "No kidding," thought Ragweed, who was busy strolling into the ever exclusive Mayberry School For Girls in Montecito, California. The school was so pretentious that it didn't even have a real address. But the school matrons did require real uniforms, with signature forest green.

And right now, coming up the Mayberry Girls School walk was a sea of Forest green leprechaun looking students heading to class. Two hundred plus young ladies in green checkered skirts, a white blouse, green blazers, green and white saddle shoes, and Ragweed's personal favorite, a green fedora hat. "Good grief!" mused Ragweed as she viewed the floating fedoras.

Of course, Ragweed was wearing her uniform, too. "At least the hat covers my hair," thought Ragweed, who had tried, once again this morning, unsuccessfully, to plaster it all down in some orderly fashion. Almost immediately her hair started springing up on its own...And as Ragweed did every morning, she squashed the little green hat on her head with a sigh and got ready to head for class. Ragweed had come upon her nickname honestly with shocks of hair that escaped description. Her Moms spent untold dollars with multiple hair salons to no avail. Ragweed's hair was her hair, and that was that.

"Another exciting day of class," mused Ragweed, who was a straight "A" student, and found most subjects quite boring. Ragweed's entire class was in the 99th percentile of students nationwide. So most of her classmates were bored as well. The new English teacher had provided some interesting moments during her initial classes. Ms. Bottswig had tried to appeal to a sense of goodness during her classes (trying to tame the disruptive bunch), talking about focusing on "reciprocity" instead of "retaliation", and other things that neither Ragweed nor her classmates had any inkling about. All the while, Mrs. Bottswig looked like she had been swigging a thing or two, on her own time. And it was not a pretty sight, to be sure.

Adventures with Ragweed

Ragweed assumed that Mrs. Bottswig hated teaching, and was in fact, scared of her students. Accordingly, Mrs. Bottswig would say bizarre things to try and trick the students into behaving correctly, instead of just telling them to sit down and be quiet. After a particularly hectic Monday class, Mrs. Bottswig suggested everybody bring a pillow and rest during class on Tuesday. Maybe Mrs. Bottswig thought resting during class would settle them down. "This woman has been eating fruit loops," mused Ragweed. "And swallowing them." Not to mention that Mrs. Bottswig's physical decline was becoming more apparent daily.

Nevertheless, the next day, with much snickering and giggling, the entire class showed up with pillows. Their parents were fairly mystified about their daughters' need to bring a pillow to school. But it was school after all, and a teacher must be obeyed, no matter how weird she may seem. The end result was not a calm class, but a gigantic pillow fight. When the Head Mistress appeared through a cloud of feathers to see what was going on, Mrs. Bottswig promptly blamed everything on her students and denied any cupability whatsoever in the melee.

The entire class earned Saturday detention, and Mrs. Bottswig earned a payback as far as Ragweed was concerned. "Right," thought Ragweed. "So this is how she plays it." Moms and Pops were mortified about their little poopsie doodle getting detention. And no matter how hard Ragweed tried to explain what had actually happened, it was so strange an event, that Ragweed finally gave up and accepted her fate. When Ragweed learned that the cost of the pillow was coming out of her allowance, it was the last straw.

So during that fun-filled Saturday detention, while weeding the school garden, which Ragweed detested, Ragweed hatched a plan. It was a grand plan. A plan she would only share with her best friend, Marney. (She had so much dirt on Marney, that any secret was safe with her.) The plot thickened. The first part of the plan was to slip out an idea, in a backhanded sort of way, in Mrs. Bottswig's Friday class, about the moving experience Ragweed had had in the school's atrium, an area that was filled with plants of all kinds, and a lovely statue of a wood nymph. Although the class looked at Ragweed as though she was a nut case, the hook was set.

On Monday morning, as if on schedule, Mrs. Bottswig announced that the class would be heading to the school's atrium to participate in an exercise of contemplation and meditation. The classroom groans were quite audible, but Ragweed and Marney just smiled at each other. And off the students traipsed, two by two, as required by Mrs. Bottswig, who looked as though she had spent the greater part of her weekend at a local bar. She was definitely becoming more unhinged every day. Maybe this would push her over the edge, and out of the school forever.

One of the things about the atrium was, that everybody had to take off their shoes upon entering. So all students dutifully and carefully took off their green and white saddle shoes, and wandered behind Mrs. Bottswig, as she said strange and forgettable things, while meandering through the atrium.

Ragweed and Marney stayed carefully at the end of the line, as was previously planned. They hid their shoes behind a rhododendron plant, so they could access them at any time, and pro-

ceeded to mix and match all the rest of twenty-one Mayberry senior class green and white oxford shoes in complete disorder. A size 5 right shoe would be with a size 7 left shoe, a size 8 with a size 6, and so on, until all was rearranged to Ragweed's satisfaction.

And then it was time to return to the classroom. No one, who was not actually present at the time, could imagine the confusion and concern raised by twenty-one senior girl students as they tried to put their shoes back on. Nothing matched. Nothing fit.

People were calling out to each other, "I have a 7 left and a 9 right. Anybody have a 7 right?" Ragweed and Marney pretended to be outraged, so no one would suspect them of any wrongdoing, and got great pleasure out of watching Mrs. Bottswig as she realized her tenure at Mayberry School was most likely coming to an end.

It took over two hours until each classmate got a pair of shoes that would fit. Parents were waiting to pick up students. And the Head Mistress was having some difficulty explaining that their daughters were busy looking for their shoes, but they would be right there. All the while, Ragweed and Marney reacted with ap-

propriate concern and amazement, as they secretly plucked their shoes from behind the rhododendron. It was a grand day, and Mrs. Bottswig eventually just disappeared…never to return.

To this day, whenever Ragweed hears the term, "If the shoe fits," she gets a knowing look on her face…but, it must be noted, that Ragweed continues to initial all her dresses, coats, shoes, socks, and even her underwear, as a protective measure.

Linda Lou Crosby

Ragweed
rides a
Horse

Beautiful purple sunsets, magnificent Saguaro Cactus, ever changing desert shapes…ah Arizona. Although Ragweed's earliest recollection of the Southwest was actually less attractive than words on that postcard…

"It'll be fun. Everybody else has done a ride," said Ragweed's friend Marney. Ragweed should have known better as Marney was always pleading with her to do things. Well, actually usually it was the other way around. But what was important was that Marney had invited Ragweed to Phoenix, Arizona for a tennis tournament. OK, fine. Ragweed would have been content with that. Couldn't she just enjoy the scenic beauty of the state like a regular person? Play some tennis. Irritate her opponents. Whatever it took. Why add horses?

Oh no, Marney had decided a moonlight horseback ride would be an added adventure for Ragweed. And Marney had already made the reservation. And everybody was doing this. And moonlight rides were sooooo much fun. "Everybody, feverybody", thought Ragweed. Ragweed was not "into" horses at the time, for obvious reasons. Oh, Ragweed had gone on plenty of horseback rides when it was daylight and nevertheless was outmatched every time by the horse. In fact, Ragweed's backside had decorated the ground of a number of western states. She had the memories to prove it.

First there was Wacko, who made it his personal goal to knock Ragweed off with low hanging branches. It was like that horse made a beeline for the perfect opportunity and lined it up with Ragweed's head. The only good thing about Wacko was he had given Ragweed a decent excuse for her hairdo, which seemed to resemble a disorganized artichoke. Hence the name Ragweed.

Then there was Bismark. "That horse could have been a boat," thought Ragweed. And in some cases he sort of was. Bismarck enjoyed water of any kind; streams, ponds, swimming pools…you name it. And Bismarck's specialty was dunking a hapless rider in any available puddle. Unfortunately Bismarck's final waterslide presentation was a mud pond, which rendered Ragweed practically unrecognizable. "Ragweed, is that you?" Ragweed's Mom had asked as Ragweed squished her way through the back door of their opulent home. "Why are you coming in by the servant's quarters?" "Did you go to the spa?" asked Moms. Ragweed was furious, mortified and smelly, and with her eyes peeping out of mud holes, Ragweed concentrated on putting one mud ball in front of the other as she tracked little muddy footprints to her room. Bismarck's whereabouts continues to be a mystery to the stable.

And of course Drowsy, who didn't move more than 20 feet from any corral. Ragweed actually thought he'd died at one point during their rather boring ride, until she heard him snore. Ragweed had to go home and get her alarm clock to come back and wake Drowsy up and get him to the barn. The stable people told Ragweed that she would have to pay double if she didn't return her horse on time. "What a racket", thought Ragweed, who's family was incredibly wealthy. It wasn't the money; it was the principle of the matter. And then the word racket reminded Ragweed of why she was really in Phoenix. And it did not have anything whatsoever to do with horses.

But nevertheless, there she was heading to the stables with Marney. If it wasn't past Ragweed's bedtime, Ragweed might have blopped Marney one right on the spot. But Ragweed was tired, and displeased and the duo arrived fashionably late for their ride. Ragweed was hoping for too late, but that didn't happen. All the other darling little midnight riders were mounted up and ready to go.

"Don't worry about us," called Ragweed. "Go right ahead without us." And Marney (who was fast becoming an ex-friend of Ragweed's) hopped up on her horse, and said, "We'll catch up." Then there was Ragweed's horse. At first glance, the horse looked a little "Paunchy," so that became the horse's name. And Paunchy also looked very unhappy to be going anywhere outside of her

corral. And appeared to have a supreme dislike both for midnight rides and her two handlers. If Ragweed wasn't in such a foul mood, she might have admired Paunchy, just a little bit.

The wranglers, whatever their names were, began to saddle Paunchy up, or attempt to. The mare didn't like that idea at all and demonstrated her displeasure by sending a swift kick to wrangler one's backside. "Ooooh", mused Ragweed, "I have never ridden a kicker before. How swell."

Apparently, the two wranglers were determined to saddle the mare, all the while Paunchy was equally determined to get back to her corral. It was quite a wreck in the making, and the dust flew. When the men sort of had the saddle on top of Paunchy, and tried to rig it up, they realized that Paunchy was too fat. The cinch looked like a postage stamp against her belly. Dufus and Dorfus (names Ragweed had now given the wranglers) looked like the western answer to Curly, Moe and Joe. Except they weren't funny. "They are idiots", realized Ragweed.

The other riders in Ragweed's 'group' had meandered off into whatever was left of the moonlight. Since it was technically a moonlight ride, Ragweed assumed the other riders were taking the ride while the moon was still available. How quaint.

Then, in a moment of surprising clarity, Dufus realized that Paunchy wasn't exactly fat; in fact she was going to have a foal. Ragweed was most amazed he'd missed that little detail, especially on one of his own horses. Ragweed had watched numerous polo matches with Moms and Pops, and she didn't remember that pregnant mares were out there running around with polo players on them. And what was good enough for a self-respecting polo player was good enough for Ragweed. She started to head back to the car.

But the undynamic duo wouldn't quit. In fact they got more determined to have Paunchy saddled. Dufus began to chew on Dorfus for bringing Paunchy (his horse) out to ride when she was obviously (after 10 minutes of figuring it out) going to have a foal. Dorfus looked at Dufus mystified (an easy task for him). "That ain't my mare. I thought she was yours." And they in turn asked all the other wranglers whose horse it was. Turned out that no one in that place had ever seen Paunchy before. No one had any idea where she came from or how she got to be in that corral. But most of them had a dim idea of how she had 'got' pregnant. And then there was a chorus of bad words that accompanied Paunchy and the two wranglers back to Paunchy's most likely temporary boarding arrangement. Ragweed was dumbfounded; the wranglers were just plain dumb.

The good news was that the moon was on the wane. "Every little minute helps," thought Ragweed. She could head back to the hotel. Of course, she needed Marney to drive her there. And Marney was still firmly planted on top of her horse, with a big, ridiculous smile on her face. "What is the matter with that girl," thought Ragweed. "She is even more irritating than I remember." Marney was going on a moonlight ride with Ragweed, and that was that. She was even tapping her irritating fingers on the saddle horn, "Let's go," said Marney, obviously forgetting that Ragweed still did not have a rideable horse.

But that changed as the two cowboy clowns actually hauled out the best horse of them all, a Mr. Pip. That was his real name.

Adventures with Ragweed

He was black, and he looked like he had a white bowtie on his chest. In fact, Ragweed thought Mr. Pip wasn't half bad. He seemed to have appropriate breeding, and turned his nose down on all present, except for Ragweed, of course. "He knows these jokers are idiots, too", thought Ragweed. "He is one smart horse." Mr. Pip was quite well behaved. "I might even have a decent time," thought Ragweed. What was left of the moonlight bounced off the cactus and the desert terrain, as Mr. Pip and Ragweed, with Marney close by, headed out into the desert. And miracle of miracles, Ragweed did not bounce off her horse. Even though Ragweed came very close multiple times, Mr. Pip would sort of move up under her to save her any undue embarrassment. The ride was actually kind of peaceful, although short. The girls got a discount because of the confusion. And, as Marney and Ragweed headed home, the sun rose.

On the ride back, Ragweed couldn't help but wonder who that pregnant mare belonged to? Ragweed didn't think someone could just misplace a 1000 lb animal, eating for two. But then, what did she know about horses? Was Mr. Pip somehow involved? Ah, the mysteries of life.

About the Author

contact: LL_neon@iwvisp.com

If you enjoyed this book, please leave me a review on Amazon. Or drop me a line, would love to hear from my readers.

Linda Lou Crosby is an Emmy nominated video producer and an award winning humor columnist and journalist. She is a member of the Dramatists Guild, the broadcast honorary, Alpha Epsilon Rho, and achieved a degree in Journalism and Broadcasting from California State College at Los Angeles.

Her life is an eclectic montage of challenge (world class tennis player, documentary producer), creativity (writer and producer of original western theater throughout California), and controlled chaos, (kayaking, fishing, swimming out of a sinking vehicle), hiking, cow punching – sometimes in Reverse - sprouting theater experiences for numerous about to be opera houses across the west, and current resident of Ingomar, Montana, population 13.

Crosby is also co-owner, with husband Hart Broesel, of Camp IOU, a place where friends (old friends and those not yet met) can come together and experience the wide-open gumbo country of Eastern Montana.

Crosby has created gardens that the Incredible Hulk could hide in, friendships that span cultures, geography and good sense, and driven her family quite wild with various uncommon ideas for adventure; up to and including snow shoeing, archery, bicycling, and improv theater; sometimes simultaneously.

With "Adventures with Ragweed", Linda Lou brings her wit and whimsy together through the eyes of a somewhat capricious and ever inventive young girl. The important thing to remember about Ragweed's adventures is that "…All characters appearing in this work are fictitious. Any resemblance to real persons, living or dead, is purely coincidental…..."

www.ingramcontent.com/pod-product-compliance
Lightning Source LLC
Chambersburg PA
CBHW042331150426
43194CB00001B/24